VISIONS OF HOPE

Activities and **Prayers** to Start a **Revival**

Author
Karen Fitzsimmons

Illustrators
Rowena Hoover, Alicia Rus,
and Anonymous

the Write Place inc

PUBLISHING + DESIGN

ISBN: 979-8-9854746-0-2

Published in the United States of America by the Write Place, Inc.
For more information, please contact:

the Write Place, Inc.
809 W. 8th Street, Suite 2
Pella, Iowa 50219
www.thewriteplace.biz

Cover and interior design by Michelle Stam, the Write Place, Inc.
Cover and interior illustrations by Rowena Hoover.
Additional interior illustrations by Alicia Rus and an anonymous artist.
Author photo and sunset photo by Jodi Kaldenberg-Rau.
Illustrator photo from personal collection.

The activities in this book are published by Karen Fitzsimmons. Please approach people with prayer and caution. Karen Fitzsimmons is not responsible for activities that could cause harm to yourself or others.

View other Write Place titles at thewriteplace.biz.

Dedication

I dedicate this book to my mom and dad.
I also thank God for His grace and goodness.
Without Him, I would not be able to do anything.
Without a doubt, the Lord is amazing.

Table of Contents

Introduction

This book is filled with engaging, faith-based activities for you to work on with your family and friends! The goal of each activity is to show someone, through an act of kindness or prayer, that they have value and purpose. With God's help, it is my hope that your actions will start a revival, spreading hope and love in your town.

The activities are organized by the place where you can complete them:

School

Church

Hospital

Nursing Home

Community

Throughout *Visions of Hope*, there are spaces where you can write down what you did. Each section includes a list of suggested prayers. The activities and prayers are intended for children and adults to work on together. Some activities involve giving out encouraging cards or sending out prayers in balloons and on scraps of paper. If you'd like, you may include the email **kalenagracewins@gmail.com** on your card or prayer. This is my email, and I'd love to hear from the people you reach! I'd also love to hear from you about your experiences with the activities in *Visions of Hope*.

This book gives ideas, but you are welcome to use your creativity and come up with your own activities. I just ask that you say a prayer before you get started. Let the Holy Spirit guide you. Remember—God gets all the glory!

Karen Fitzsimmons

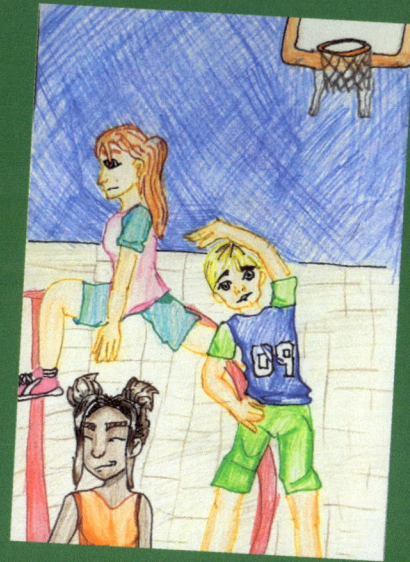

SCHOOL

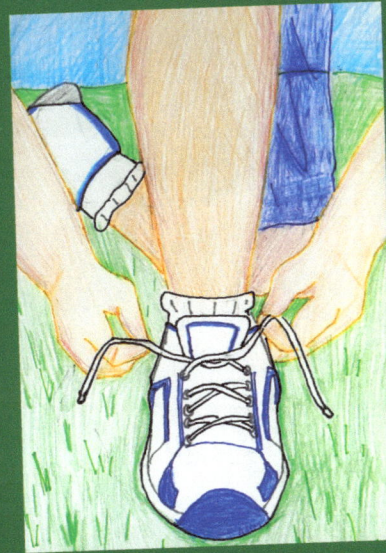

Color student illustrations by Alicia Rus. Black and white student illustration by Anonymous.

Activities

Help someone with their schoolwork.

Bake a plate of cookies to share with students, teachers, or staff members.

Sit by someone at lunch or in the hallway who looks like they need a friend.

Say hello to a student
and ask, "How are you?"
Listen to their answer.

Start a conversation with
someone at school whom you've
never talked to before.

Learn ten students' names.
Say hello to each of them by name.

If you are a student, get to class early and ask your teacher how they are doing.

Compliment or encourage a teacher or another staff member.

Compliment or encourage a student.

If you hear someone being negative about something, gently remind them to be positive.

If you hear someone being mean, kindly ask them to stop. We should all avoid talking badly about others!

Tell someone about Jesus' love.

Journal about what you did...

_____
_____
_____
_____
_____
_____
_____
_____
_____
_____
_____
_____
_____
_____

Ask someone at school how they want to make a difference in the world.

If you witness bullying, report it to a teacher, a principal, or another authority figure.

Take a walk with your camera and a friend and take pictures of sunsets—God's beauty!

Photo by Jodi Kaldenberg-Rau

If someone at school has hurt you, tell that person, "I forgive you for _____." Let it go! If you have hurt someone, tell them you are sorry. Ask if they will forgive you. Even if they will not, you should feel good that you tried and that you let the anger go.

If someone at school looks sad or lonely, ask if they need a prayer. Then say a prayer for them.

_____
_____
_____
_____
_____
_____
_____
_____
_____
_____
_____
_____
_____
_____
_____
_____
_____

Gather a group of friends and pray together before school.

During lunchtime, start a Bible group for anyone who wants to join.

Prayers

Pray when you have free
time during the school day.
Talk to God in your thoughts
or write to Him in your journal.

When you walk past the lockers,
pray that each student finds Jesus.

Pray for God to be brought
back into the schools.

_____
_____
_____
_____
_____
_____
_____
_____
_____
_____
_____
_____
_____
_____
_____
_____
_____

_____
_____
_____
_____
_____
_____
_____
_____
_____
_____
_____
_____
_____
_____
_____
_____

Pray that students, teachers, and staff will be safe from harm at school.

Pray that the secretaries will act with guidance and wisdom.

Pray for a revival in the schools.

Pray that the next generation will be strong and pass on the truth about Jesus to their families and friends.

Pray for the safety of the bus drivers and the students who ride the bus. Also pray that everyone on the bus will be calm and respectful.

Pray that bullies will be inspired to be kind and treat others with respect.

Write a prayer...

_____
_____
_____
_____
_____
_____
_____
_____
_____
_____
_____
_____
_____
_____
_____

Pray for students who have been bullied or who are very sad. Pray that God will reach them and give them hope.

Pray that principals and administrators will show each student that they are important and are making a difference.

CHURCH

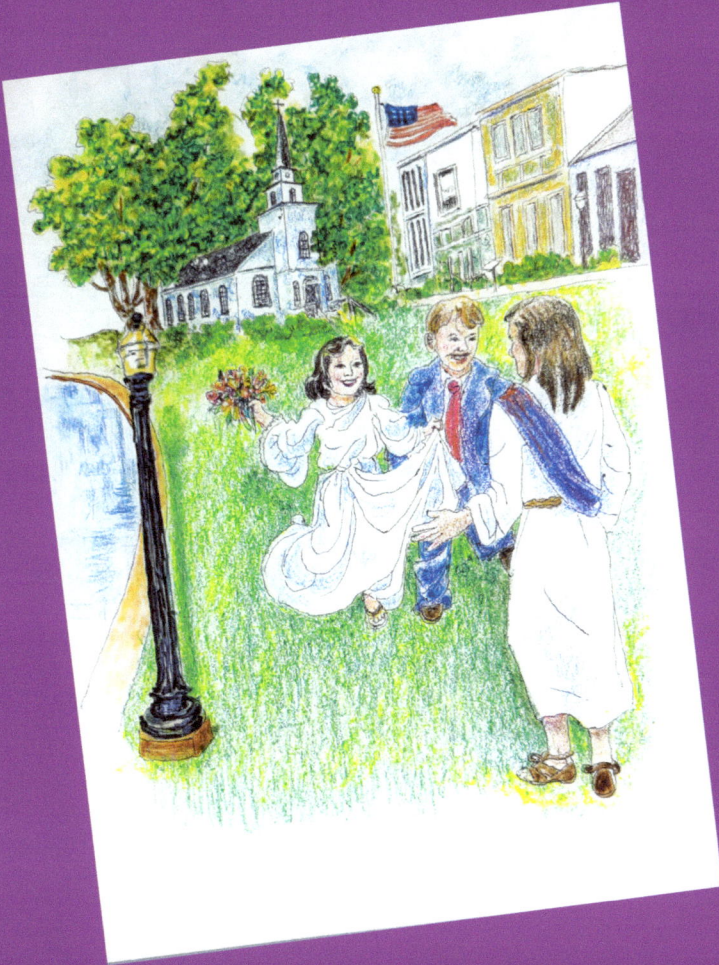

Activities

Ask someone at your church when they accepted Jesus.

Draw pictures and write encouraging messages on them. Hang the pictures up somewhere in the church or give them to someone.

Gather a group of friends or family and take turns reading one of your favorite chapters or stories in the Bible. Talk about it together.

Ask someone at church, "How are you?" Listen to their answer.

Make a card and give it to a church leader to send to someone who needs kind words.

_____

_____

_____

_____

_____

_____

_____

_____

_____

_____

_____

_____

_____

Smile and say hello to someone at church whom you've never talked to before.

Play a word guessing game at church! One person will pick a secret word, and the rest of the group will ask ten questions about it. They will try to guess what the word is based on the answers. Here are some word ideas: FAITH, LOVE, CROSS, COURAGE.

Play a compliment game! Everyone will write their name on a poster and draw a picture of themselves. Then, the group will pass the posters around. When you get a poster, write something nice about the person on it.

Recite a favorite Bible verse to someone and explain why you like it.

_____
_____
_____
_____
_____
_____
_____
_____
_____
_____
_____
_____
_____
_____

_____
_____
_____
_____
_____
_____
_____
_____
_____
_____
_____
_____
_____
_____
_____

Brainstorm a way to raise money for a charity. Share your idea with a church leader.

Have a scavenger hunt at church! Find objects that start with a "J," an "E," an "S," a "U," and another "S." (Hint: You're spelling JESUS!)

Have another scavenger hunt! But this time, spell out "GOD IS LOVE" with the objects.

Sing a song you learned at church with someone. **If** they don't know the song, teach it to them!

Form a prayer group and pray about anything that is placed on your heart.

Ask everyone in the church or youth group to join hands and pray for a revival.

_____
_____
_____
_____
_____
_____
_____
_____
_____
_____
_____
_____
_____
_____
_____

Prayers

Pray that the church staff will be full of compassion and won't turn away anyone who approaches them because of their appearance, age, or past. Pray that the church staff will see every conversation as an opportunity. Jesus died on the cross for all—we are not to choose who is or is not included in our church body.

When you stand at the church's entrance, pray that anyone who enters will feel welcomed by the people inside.

Pray that the elderly at church will be respected and that the young will not be overlooked.

Pray for anyone at church who is having a hard time.

Write a prayer...

_____
_____
_____
_____
_____
_____
_____
_____
_____
_____
_____
_____
_____
_____

Pray for nations to stand strong for the Lord.

When you walk around the outside of the church, pray that anyone who sees it will want to come in and talk to God.

When someone at church is unwell, pray over them, releasing the healing power of Jesus.

Pray that ministers will give sermons of truth and let the Holy Spirit guide them. Stand in the exact spot where the minister gives sermons as you are praying.

People often talk to ministers about the things that worry them. When you stand by a minister's office, pray that they will not become stressed or overwhelmed by the worries of the congregation, or the worries of people outside the congregation.

23

Pray that more people will turn to God themselves instead of always asking a minister to pray for them.

The world is full of unforgiveness. Pray that families will reunite and forgive one another.

Pray that everyone in the church body forgives one another. Also pray that people forgive themselves for their past sins.

Ask the Holy Spirit to lead you to anyone at church who is sad. Talk to them and ask if you can pray with them.

Pray for the children of the church. Ask that each generation will be stronger than the last.

Pray that everyone in the church knows that when God chooses you, it doesn't matter who else has rejected you.

Pray that non-believers and Christians will come together to worship the one True God.

When you have planted the seed of Jesus' love with someone, pray that God will lead you to someone else who needs Him.

HOSPITAL

Activities

Start a conversation with someone
in the waiting room at the hospital.

Help someone open a door.

With permission from the hospital,
get a bowl of fruit or a plate of
cookies and pass the treats
out to the patients and staff.

Write an encouraging note and ask a nurse to hand it to someone.

Visit someone in the hospital. Talk to them about why they are there and listen to their story.

Compliment a nurse, a doctor, or someone else on the hospital staff.

Compliment a patient.

Give a flower to someone who
could use encouragement.

Read to or pray for a patient.

Start a game in the waiting room.

Listen to a patient's story about happy times. Tell them a story about you.

Smile and say hello when you pass people in the hallway.

Ask a staff member or patient how they're doing. Make sure you listen to their answer.

Make someone laugh or smile.

Buy a balloon for a patient.

If you see someone crying in the hospital, ask if they would like to talk or pray with you.

Have a cup of coffee or ice water with a patient or a staff member. Sit and talk with them.

With permission from the hospital, set up a little corner table with a sign asking if anyone needs prayers. If someone stops, pray with them.

If you love animals, look into training a service animal who can visit with patients at the hospital.

Get blankets or flowers and pray over them. Then give them to whomever the Holy Spirit tells you needs them at the hospital.

Go to the café in the hospital and buy a meal for whomever the Holy Spirit puts on your heart.

Write prayers in cards and give them to patients or anyone at the hospital who looks like they need a prayer.

Write down Bible verses and leave them in certain spots around the hospital.

Prayers

Walk in the halls, praying for the patients.

Pray blessings over the nurses
as they walk past you.

35

Pray for healing. If you are feeling brave, pray for healing out loud, giving God all the credit and glory.

Pray that forgiveness will touch every person you see at the hospital. We waste so much time not forgiving ourselves or others!

Pray that the doctors will have compassion and wisdom.

Pray for people who have an addiction. Feel free to witness and share testimonies, knowing that only God is the judge—not people.

_____
_____
_____
_____
_____
_____
_____
_____
_____
_____
_____
_____
_____
_____
_____
_____
_____
_____

Write a prayer...

_____

_____

_____

_____

_____

_____

_____

_____

_____

_____

_____

_____

_____

_____

_____

When you have planted the seed of Jesus' love with someone, pray that God will lead you to someone else who needs Him.

NURSING HOME

Childhood Memories

Activities

_____
_____
_____
_____
_____
_____
_____
_____
_____
_____
_____
_____
_____
_____
_____
_____

Ask a resident at a nursing home for advice and listen to their wisdom. Journal their answer if you want to— you may use their advice someday!

Listen to a resident's story about their life. If it's okay with the resident, journal about their story while they talk.

Ask someone at the nursing home how they are. Listen to their answer.

Smile and say hello as you pass people in the hallways.

Volunteer to help out with a class or to read to someone.

Ask someone to show you pictures from their life and tell you about them.

_____
_____
_____
_____
_____
_____
_____
_____
_____
_____
_____
_____
_____
_____
_____
_____

Journal about what you did...

_____
_____
_____
_____
_____
_____
_____
_____
_____
_____
_____
_____
_____
_____

Find a couple living at the nursing home and ask how they met.

Open a door for someone.

Give a balloon to someone.

Share words of encouragement with someone.

Color with someone.

Help put a jigsaw puzzle together or help with a crossword puzzle.

Ask someone if they would like you to pray with them or just listen while they pray.

Play cards or a board game
with someone.

Gather a group of friends and write
prayers on cards Then deliver the
cards to whomever the Holy Spirit
guides you to at the nursing home.
You can hand the cards out or place
them at residents' doors.

Ask a resident to pray for you out loud because you need their prayer.

Invite residents to write prayers down on strips of paper with you. On a windy day, let the prayers go. Ask the Holy Spirit to carry the prayers to the right hands.

Prayers

_____
_____
_____
_____
_____
_____
_____
_____
_____
_____
_____
_____
_____
_____

Pray that nursing home residents will share their stories with anyone who will listen. Pray that the people who listen will learn from the residents' mistakes and successes.

Pray that the staff and residents at the nursing home will be safe and protected.

Pray that young people will come from all walks of life to get advice from elderly people who love the Lord.

Pray that the caregivers will love and give quality care to the residents.

If a nursing home is understaffed, pray that the caregivers will feel encouraged and that they won't give up.

Write a prayer...

_____

_____

_____

_____

_____

_____

_____

_____

_____

_____

_____

_____

_____

_____

_____

Pray for the Holy Spirit to guide you to people in need of encouragement at the nursing home.

Pray that residents will appreciate their caregivers and show compassion if mistakes are made.

Pray that residents' faith will grow as time goes on.

Pray that the people in nursing homes will know they are loved by Jesus and still have a purpose.

Pray that residents will not be fearful to witness for the Lord.

Pray that residents will live fearlessly! Pray that they will not be afraid to live outside the box for the Lord.

_____
_____
_____
_____
_____
_____
_____
_____
_____
_____
_____
_____
_____
_____
_____
_____

Write a prayer...

_____
_____
_____
_____
_____
_____
_____
_____
_____
_____
_____
_____
_____
_____
_____
_____
_____
_____

Pray that residents will form prayer groups and Bible studies at the nursing home.

Pray for the people in nursing homes who have lost a loved one. Pray that they will not give in to sadness, but instead make the most out of the time they have to witness for the Lord.

Pray that nursing home staff and administrators will show compassion and not feel stressed.

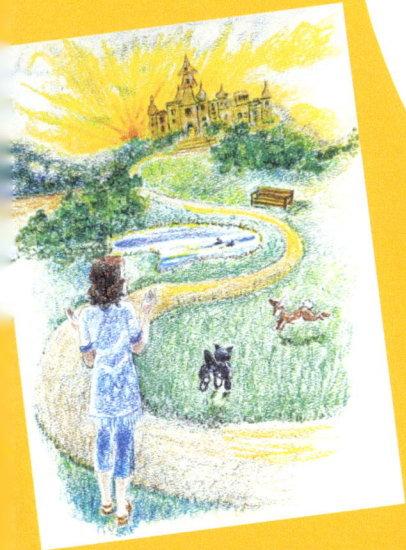

COMMUNITY

Activities

When waiting in line at a store, let someone go in front of you.

If you are driving and notice a car that needs to turn or a person who needs to cross, let them go ahead of you if it is safe to do so. (Or ask the driver to do that!)

Open the door for someone.

If you see someone with a pet, ask them questions or compliment their pet.

Ask someone in your neighborhood how they are. Then make sure you listen to their answer.

Set flowers by someone's door with a positive note.

Go for a walk and smile and say hello to the people you pass.

Hand someone a flower and wish them a nice day.

Share an encouraging word with someone or compliment them.

Buy someone a coffee,
a milkshake, or a meal.

Pay for someone's groceries.

Go to a coffee shop and give the
cashier $20 or more. Tell them
you would like to pay for everyone
behind you until the money runs out.

Journal about what you did...

_____

_____

_____

_____

_____

_____

_____

_____

_____

_____

_____

_____

_____

_____

_____

If you see someone who looks sad, talk to the person or pray for them.

Have a picnic or play a game in a public place where you could meet new friends.

Wear a t-shirt that says, "Free Hugs." Give a hug to anyone who asks!

Hand out bottles of water at a community event.

Write prayers on little pieces of paper, put them in balloons, and let the wind take them.

Start a conversation with someone about Jesus. Let the Holy Spirit guide you on whom to talk to and when.

Prayers

Pray when you have free time during the school day. Talk to God in your thoughts or write to Him in your journal.

Walk around town. If you feel the need to pray in a certain spot, stop and pray.

Walk into a grocery store and pray for anyone God tugs on your heart to notice. Pray for Jesus' love to pour on them.

When you walk past a hospital or nursing home, pray for healing and for the patients to find Jesus.

Pray for every church you see. Let the Holy Spirit guide you.

Write a prayer...

_____

_____

_____

_____

_____

_____

_____

_____

_____

_____

_____

_____

_____

_____

_____

_____

Write a prayer...

_____
_____
_____
_____
_____
_____
_____
_____
_____
_____
_____
_____
_____
_____
_____

Pray that each person who walks past you will know Jesus and have a personal relationship with Him.

When you walk past houses, pray the families will stay strong in the Lord.

When you are in a restaurant, ask your server, "How can we pray for you?" Listen and pray for them.

When you walk past a park, pray for the safety of the children who play there.

If you hear a siren, pray for healing and that the person in trouble knows the truth about Jesus.

When you see a movie theater, pray for Jesus' love and protection for the people inside.

_____

_____

_____

_____

_____

_____

_____

_____

_____

_____

_____

_____

_____

_____

_____

_____

Write a prayer...

_____

_____

_____

_____

_____

_____

_____

_____

_____

_____

_____

_____

If you walk past a college, pray that the young adults will make wise choices and find personal relationships with Jesus.

When you see a car go by, pray for protection and wisdom for the driver and passengers.

Pray for every school you see.

If you walk past a fire station or police station, pray that the firefighters and officers will have wisdom and protection.

_____

_____

_____

_____

_____

_____

_____

_____

_____

_____

_____

_____

_____

_____

About the Author

Karen Fitzsimmons has written many books, including *Listen My Children, Perfect Love Casts Out Fear, Angel Meets Trouble, The Secret of Happiness, The Joy of Forgiveness, Will You Be My Friend?/Serás tú mi amigo?, Don't Look Back, We Need You Jesus!, Unfailing Love,* and now *Visions of Hope: Activities and Prayers to Start a Revival.*

Karen is an art teacher and is completing her master's degree in counseling and art therapy. She is also a mother who knows how important it is to listen and show anyone she meets that they have value and that God loves them. There is an eternity waiting, so it is important to choose the right path. Whatever your age, God has a purpose for you.

Karen was inspired to become an author by her creativity and love for Jesus.

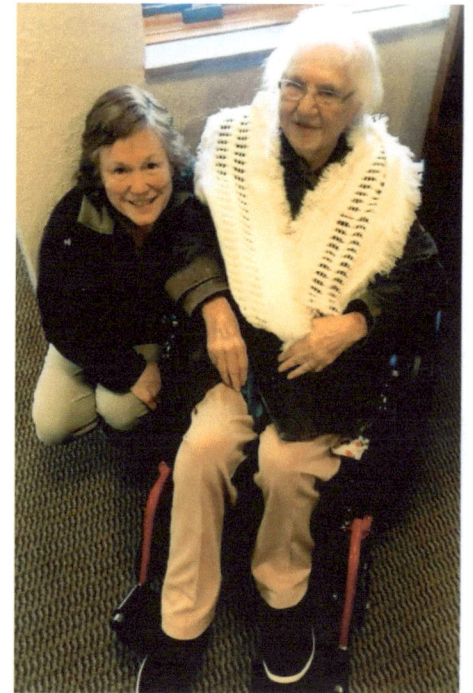

About the Illustrator

Born in Mishawaka, Indiana, in 1927, Rowena Hoover has followed in the artistic footprints of her maternal grandmother and two uncles. She majored in Art at Asbury College in Wilmore, Kentucky, and attended what was then called Iowa State Teacher's College in Cedar Falls. She was a United Methodist pastor's wife and played piano and organ. She also taught youth Sunday school classes and adult Bible studies in various locations.

Rowena helped raise two daughters and a son. She has taught adult education evening art classes, as well as classes in her own home. She has exhibited her work in galleries and other venues over the years. She also illustrated a set of First Ladies of America and their gowns, as well as a children's fairy story written by her mother. In addition to *Visions of Hope: Activities and Prayers to Start a Revival*, Rowena illustrated *Listen My Children*, *Angel Meets Trouble*, *The Secret of Happiness*, *The Joy of Forgiveness*, *Will You Be My Friend?/¿Serás tú mi amigo?*, *Don't Look Back*, and *We Need You Jesus!* by Karen Fitzsimmons.

www.ingramcontent.com/pod-product-compliance
Lightning Source LLC
Chambersburg PA
CBHW040713150426

42813CB00061B/2976